Reading Level: 4–5
Interest Level: 4–6

Complete Set of 4 books:
$110.40/**$82.80**
ISBN: 978-1-5382-8161-1
Individual Titles: $27.60/**$20.70**
Specs: 32 pp., 8 ½" x 11", Full-Color Photographs

- Diagrams show how to operate different kinds of technology
- Touches on key STEM concepts
- Incorporates laws about and potential problems of new technology

SCIENCE TECHNOLOGY

The Tech-Head Guide

Technology development moves at a breakneck pace. But understanding how inventions and innovations began can help later comprehension of new technology. This set does just that: It explains the beginnings of computers, drones, artificial intelligence, and robots, bringing readers to the present cutting edge through real-life examples and full-color photographs. In this set, readers get an idea of what could come next too, like drones delivering medicines in rural locations. While comprehensive, the text is written with young readers in mind and with an enthusiasm that allows anyone to get excited about the technology that's to come.

			Library Bound Book	eBook	©
1	**AI** (William Potter) Dewey: • GRL: R • ATOS: PENDING	GS7689 ①	978-1-5382-7739-3	978-1-5382-7740-9	©2023
2	**Computers** (William Potter) Dewey: • GRL: R • ATOS: PENDING	GS7690 ②	978-1-5382-7743-0	978-1-5382-7744-7	©2023
3	**Drones** (William Potter) Dewey: • GRL: R • ATOS: PENDING	GS7691 ③	978-1-5382-7747-8	978-1-5382-7748-5	©2023
4	**Robots** (William Potter) Dewey: • GRL: R • ATOS: PENDING	GS7692 ④	978-1-5382-7751-5	978-1-5382-7752-2	©2023

① GS7689   ② GS7690   ③ GS7691   ④ GS7692

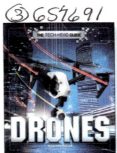

new for FALL

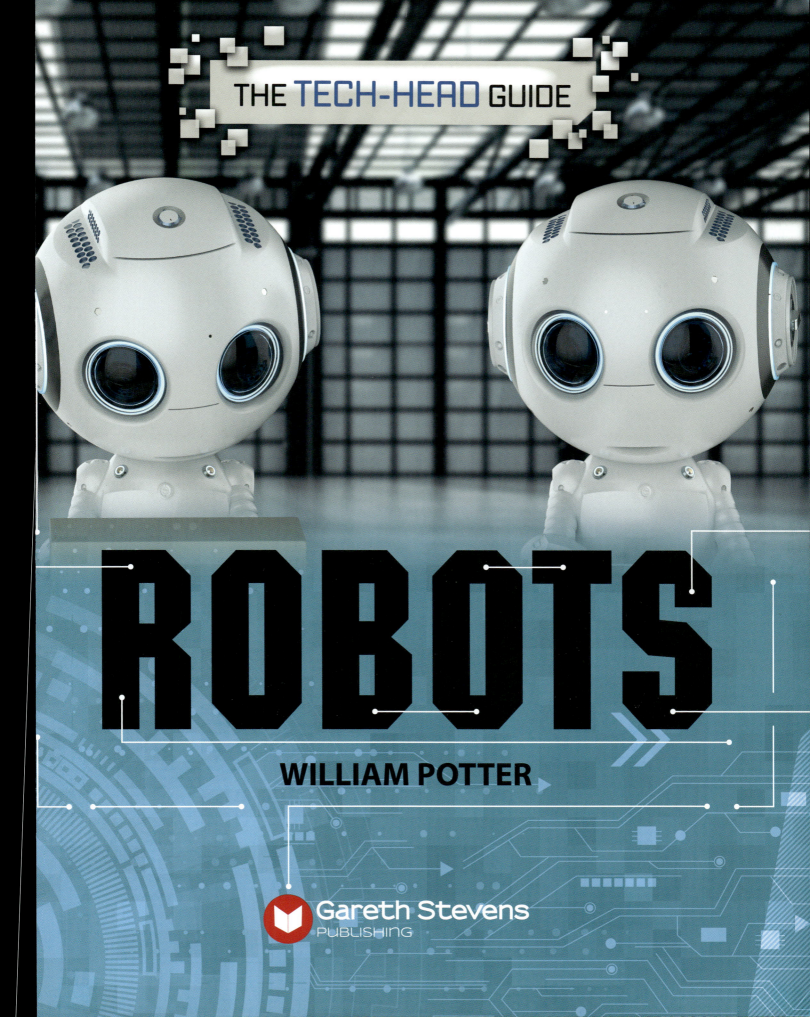

THE TECH-HEAD GUIDE

ROBOTS

WILLIAM POTTER

Gareth Stevens
PUBLISHING

Please visit our website, www.garethstevens.com. For a free color catalog of all our high-quality books, call toll free 1-800-542-2595 or fax 1-877-542-2596.

Cataloging-in-Publication Data
Names: Potter, William.
Title: Robots / William Potter.
Description: New York : Gareth Stevens Publishing, 2023. | Series: The tech-head guide | Includes glossary and index.
Identifiers: ISBN 9781538277492 (pbk.) | ISBN 9781538277515 (library bound) | ISBN 9781538277508 (6pack) | ISBN 9781538277522 (ebook)
Subjects: LCSH: Robots--Juvenile literature. | Robotics--Juvenile literature.
Classification: LCC TJ211.2 P688 2023 | DDC 629.8'92--dc23

Published in 2023 by
Gareth Stevens Publishing
29 E. 21st Street
New York, NY 10010

Editor: Elise Short
Design concept: Wild Pixel Ltd
Designer: Jason Billin

Picture Credits

Alamy: AF Archive/WALL-E, 2008/Disney 27b; Atlaspix/Star Wars, 1977/LucasFilm/Disney 26br; Chronicle 6-7bg, 6bl, 7b; Pictorial Press 4cl; Pictorial Press/I Robot ,2004 /20th c Fox 27t; RP Library 24cr; Sportsphoto/I Robot, 2004/20th c Fox 26-27bg; Amin Wiegel/dpa 24b.Getty Images: AFP 21cr; Bloomberg 19r; Larry Burrow/The LIFE Collection 8c; John B Carnett 16c; Koichi Kamoshidda 25b; Science & Society PL 6br, 9tl. NASA: GM 19br; JPL 8-9bg, 9cr; JPL-Caltech 5b, 25c; JSC 28r. 123RF: Dmitry Azarov: 25t. Science Photo Library: Peter Menzel 22bl, Shutterstock: AlexLMX 11cl; Anatolir 9ccl; BigMouse 8br; davooda 8bc; Patrick Daxonbichier. 11t; Mike Dotta 11br; Nor Gal 11cr; Anton Gvozdikov 23bl; Volodymyr Horbovyy 4-5bg; Imagine China/Rex 20br; Iryna Art 16-17bg; AKKHARAT JARUSILAWONG 7c; Jenson 4b; Sergey Klopotov 29bl; ksenvitain 8c; kts design back cover br,10-11bg; kuroksta 9cr; Mario's Studio 8cr; Mr Rashad 9bcr; Bas Nastassia 10cl; Titov Nikolai 9br; 90 miles 9bc; oakkii 8bl; Jurik Peter front cover b/g; Phonlamai Photo 1, 2-3bg, 9c, 29br; Quality Stock Arts 14bl, quangmoo 15b;Quinennip 9ccr; Salarew Rutso 20-21bg; Supphachai Salaeman 22-23bg, 30-31bg; SHIN-db 14-15bg; Ned Snowman 4cr; sobinsergey84 28-29bg; sripfoto 24-25 bg; suesse 8cr; Vika Suh front cover main, 29tl; temp-64GTX 29r; Tinxi 23t; TRMK 18-19bg; Usasuk 21tr; Vernonchick_84 8cl; Visual Intermezzo 12-13bg; weera.otp 10br; Xinhua/Rex 13cr; Olga Zakharova 9cl. Superstock: World History Archive/ARPL: 26bl. Wikimedia Commons: Marshall Astor from San Pedro, US/CC Wikimedia Commons 2 9tc; Nevit Dilmen/CC Wikimedia Commons 3 10cl; Erik Möller/PD Wikimedia Commons 7tl; Rama/CC Wikimedia Commons 4/Musée d'Art et d'Histoire de Neuchâtel. 7tr; U.S. Navy photo by Mass Communication Specialist 2nd Class Jhi L.Scott/Released/PD/Wikimedia Commons 12bl. Other photos courtesy of: AvatarMind back cover bl, 22br; Boston Dynamics 15cl, 23br; Caterpillar 20bl; Eelume Ekstabilde tekst 14cr; Istituto Italiano di Tecnologia (IIT) 13b; Marsi Bionics 15tr; Mesa Robotics 15b; MIT Senseable City Lab and Alm Lab 13cl; MOD ©Crown Copyright 2012.OGL back cover tr, 17tr; © QinetiQ North America MAARS 5t; 17b; Rethink Robotics Inc 18b; Robotics UK, ABB Ltd 19bl; Serbot Swiss Innovations 21cl; TATRC 17tc;

Copyright © Hodder and Stoughton, 2020

All rights reserved. No part of this book may be reproduced in any form without permission in writing from the publisher, except by a reviewer.

Printed in the United States of America

CPSIA compliance information: Batch #CSGS23: For further information contact Gareth Stevens, New York, New York at 1-800-542-2595.

Find us on

CONTENTS

ROBOTS RULE! 4
AGE OF THE AUTOMATON 6
ROBOTS FOR REAL 8
BUILD A BOT 10
DANGER DROIDS 12
MOBILE MACHINES 14
BATTLEFIELD BOTS 16
MOTOR INDUSTRY 18
ROBOT REPLACEMENTS 20
AWESOME ANDROIDS 22
MECHANICAL MEGASTARS 24
ELECTRIC DREAMS 26
THE NEXT UPGRADE 28
GLOSSARY 30
FOR MORE INFORMATION 31
INDEX 32

ROBOTS RULE!

Robots are machines that can be programmed to follow complex instructions. Some, such as the giant robotic arms used in the motor industry, are designed to do repetitive tasks, while others appear more human-like. Robots are becoming part of our daily lives, while also helping scientists explore the deepest oceans and outer space.

ROBOT NO. 1

The word **robot** comes from the Slavic word "robota" for forced laborer. It was used to describe artificial humans in the play *R.U.R* (Rossum's Universal Robots) by the Czech writer **Karel Čapek** in 1920 before being used for many kinds of automatic machines.

HELLO, HUMAN!

Robots are becoming more and more commonplace. In the home, floors are being swept by robot cleaners, while children play and learn with robotic toys. Robots are welcoming guests to hotels and offices, and providing security in train stations and airports.

ASSEMBLY LINE

Where jobs are repetitive, require strength or involve some danger, robots are the perfect tools. They don't get bored or require any rest – only maintenance. Long lines of robotic arms help build cars in assembly plants, accurately repeating the same task, day and night.

MICROBOTS

Robots are getting smaller too. Some can be programmed to work together in "**swarms**" just like worker bees. These simple machines can communicate with each other using infrared signals, and complete tasks one could not easily do on its own, such as searching large areas and pollinating crops. On the microscopic scale, tiny **nanobots** (see page 25) could soon be working to locate and fight cancer cells in the human body.

TECH WAR

The military are using robots for surveillance, to dispose of explosive devices and rescue soldiers in the battlefield. But, robots are also being used as weapons, with remote-controlled aerial robot drones able to carry bombs and self-driving tanks taking on the enemy.

ASTRO-BOTS

Exploring the planet Mars, like NASA's **Curiosity Rover**, and speeding beyond the edge of our solar system, robots are investigating places too far and too inhospitable for humans to reach. Robots are pioneers, making new discoveries and sending back data to scientists on Earth.

AGE OF THE AUTOMATON

Before the word "robot" was coined or the invention of electric power, humans built machines to perform tasks. These puppet-like creations, or **automatons**, were powered by steam or clockwork.

POWERED PIGEON

Ancient Greek engineers and mathematicians came up with plans for water-powered clocks with moving figures and even a steam-powered pigeon. This wooden bird, designed by **Archytas** (428–347 BCE), had an animal's bladder inside, which was pumped full of steam until the pigeon took off to soar for several hundred feet. It is considered to be the first self-flying machine and even the first robot.

TIME MACHINE

In 1094, Chinese inventor **Su Song** designed a towering, water-powered astronomical clock that had a rotating drum with pegs that triggered percussion sounds and moving figurines that played bells and gongs.

ROBO-KNIGHT

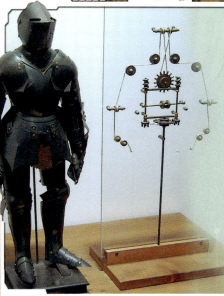

Italian Renaissance genius **Leonardo da Vinci** had his own plans for an automaton. He designed and may have built a frame of gears and pulleys to animate a suit of armor for a show in 1495. The robot knight could stand, sit, raise its visor, and move its arms.

AMAZING MANNEQUINS

Built as an advertising gimmick to sell watches in 1774, the **automatons** of Swiss watchmaker **Pierre Jaquet-Droz** are mannequins, each with up to 6,000 moving parts. They can write, draw different pictures and play an organ. The organ-playing figure even mimics breathing.

PUPPET MASTER

Karakuri are traditional Japanese puppets made from the 17th to 19th centuries. Some were designed for the theater or religious ceremonies, others served tea and bowed. The mechanized figures are powered by a wound spring that turns carved wooden gears.

MUSICAL MARVEL

The flute-playing automaton of 18th-century inventor **Jacques de Vaucanson** was almost too realistic, with artificial skin on the hands. The automaton blew air over its flute and moved its fingers to play a tune, just as a human would. The flute player was such a success, Vaucanson built two more – a tambourine player and a digesting duck that pooped!

ROBOTS FOR REAL

Clockwork models that were mostly entertaining objects were replaced by electronic robots that could be programmed to do different tasks in the 20th century. The first android robots were sensations, touring the world like celebrities. But, by the 1950s, these were replaced by more practical designs for industry, science and space exploration.

TURTLE TECH

The first self-controlling or **autonomous** robots were built by **William Grey Walter** in 1948. His slow-moving, three-wheeled bots, **Elmer** and **Elsie**, were compared to tortoises. The machines had touch and light-sensitive controls, which helped them avoid obstacles and find their way back to a recharging station.

ROBO-REPORT
Model: Sojourner
Built by: NASA, USA
Year: 1997
Role: Mars exploration
Weight: 24 pounds (11.5 kg)
Speed: 0.015 mph (0.024 kph)
Tools: Imaging Cameras, Alpha Proton X-Ray Spectrometer

TIMELINE

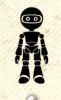 **Elektro the Moto Man** performs at the New York World Fair

 Unimate, the first digital, programmable robot, used by General Motors

 WABOT I, first human-sized, human-like robot

 Dante II walking robot collects samples from volcano

 AIBO robotic dog

1928 — **1939** — **1948** — **1954** — **1966** — **1973** — **1988** — **1994** — **1997** — **1999**

 W.H. Richards' exhibition robots, **Eric** and **George**

 First electric autonomous robots, **Elmer** and **Elsie**

 Shakey, mobile robot with vision system

 Helpmate robot used at Danbury Hospital

 NASA **Pathfinder** rover lands on Mars

NEW WORLDS

In 1997, NASA successfully landed their robot spacecraft **Pathfinder** on Mars, along with its six-wheeled Sojourner rover. This wheeled robot, powered by solar cells, traveled over 328 feet (100 m), tested soil samples, and sent pictures and information about Mars's landscape back to Earth over its 85 days of operation (12 times longer than expected). Fellow rovers **Opportunity** and **Curiosity** are still exploring the surface of Mars, looking for evidence of ancient life.

JOBS FOR ROBOTS

The robotics industry came of age in 1954 when US inventor **George Devol** introduced **Unimate** to the motor industry. This first digital and programmable robotic arm was used in 1961 at General Motors' metal-moulding plant in Trenton, New Jersey, USA, to lift and stack hot pieces of metal. Within two years, 450 Unimate robotic arms were working in the industry.

SHAKEY START

The first mobile robot able to understand its surroundings was developed by the Stanford Research Institute in the USA between 1966 and 1972. A tall and wobbly four-wheeled robot, **Shakey** was programmed to work out a route, push objects out of its path, turn lights on and off, and open and close doors. Shakey took instructions from a room-sized computer brain via a radio link, and used **sonar** and a bump sensor to avoid collisions.

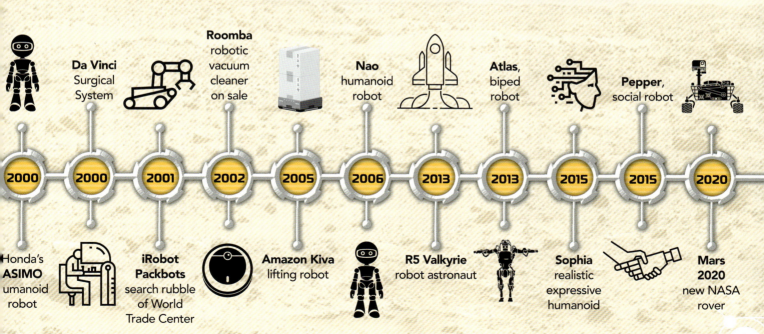

- 2000 — Honda's ASIMO umanoid robot
- 2000 — Da Vinci Surgical System
- 2001 — iRobot Packbots search rubble of World Trade Center
- 2002 — Roomba robotic vacuum cleaner on sale
- 2005 — Amazon Kiva lifting robot
- 2006 — Nao humanoid robot
- 2013 — R5 Valkyrie robot astronaut
- 2013 — Atlas, biped robot
- 2015 — Sophia realistic expressive humanoid
- 2015 — Pepper, social robot
- 2020 — Mars 2020 new NASA rover

BUILD A BOT

While robots come in many shapes and sizes, they share many of the same components – a power source, control system, sensors, and tools. Here's what you need to build your own basic robot.

MAKING SENSE

Just as we use our senses to comprehend our environment, robots use electronic **sensors** to know about their surroundings. Some sensors check the position and speed of the robot's moving parts. If the robot needs to grip or lift an object, the sensors will help it decide how much pressure or effort is required.

A mobile robot needs to know when there are obstacles in its path. Some robots simply bump into an object, then work out a path around it. Others use an **ultrasonic sensor**, firing a high-pitched sound wave, then measuring its echo, like bats. Light Detection and Ranging (**LiDAR**) works in a similar way but uses low-power lasers to measure distance. A local version of **GPS** called Simultaneous Localization and Mapping (**SLAM**) can be used for recording the robot's position.

CONTROL CENTER

The robot's **Central Processing Unit (CPU)** is its computer "brain." The CPU is where it receives commands from its operator, collects data from its sensors and instructs its body and tools to move and complete tasks. For a mobile robot, the CPU instructs a motor controller that directs a robot's movements and speed.

ELECTRONIC EYE

To record and monitor a robot's movements, a video camera is essential. A webcam allows you to stream what the robot is seeing on to a computer. More sophisticated robots carry infrared cameras that see heat signatures – changes of temperature that reveal living creatures in the dark.

POWER PACK

All robots require a power source – usually a battery of some sort. The robots that work on the surface of Mars recharge their batteries through solar cells.

TOOLS FOR THE JOB

Assembly-line robots may have just one arm with a tool for a specific task, such as drilling or welding. The human-like hands of the test robot **iCub** (2004) have sensors on the fingertips and palms to help the robot grip an object.

The **Da Vinci Surgical System** robotic arms (see page 21) use a variety of tools, such as scalpels, scissors or gripping tools, called graspers, for use in highly accurate operations, as directed by human surgeons.

LOCOMOTION

Components called **actuators** translate commands into movements. The actuators can instruct a wheel to turn or a robotic arm to move back, forwards or twist.

DANGER DROIDS

Robots are the perfect tools for working in harsh environments or dealing with extreme risk, temperatures or radioactivity where humans would face great danger if they dared to follow.

BOMB BOT

The battle-tested **PackBot** is designed for bomb disposal, surveillance and reconnaissance. It can squeeze through narrow passages and even descend stairs on its caterpillar tracks, while sending a live video feedback to its operator's tablet controller. PackBots were the first visitors to the damaged Fukushima nuclear plant in Japan after the 2011 earthquake and tsunami.

ROBO-REPORT
Model: PackBot
Built by: iRobot, USA
Year: 2002
Role: Bomb-disposal, surveillance, reconnaissance
Weight: 24 pounds (11 kg)
Speed: 5.8 miles (9.3 kph)
Sensors: 4 day-and-night cameras, two-way audio
Tools: Manipulator arm

DIRTY WORK

It's a dirty job but someone's got to do it! **Luigi** is a robot designed by Massachusetts Institute of Technology (MIT in Boston, USA) in 2015 to be lowered into sewers and gather samples of human waste – yes, poo! Scientists at MIT use the samples provided by Luigi to monitor the health of city dwellers, check diabetes levels, and identify antibiotic-resistant bacteria. Luigi carries a motor, pump, and filter to sift through the samples it finds.

UNDER PRESSURE

The pressures in the deep oceans would crush a human. We can only venture to the depths in submersibles, but robots can explore with fewer risks. The National Oceanography Center **(NOC) robots** are submarines that can survive in depths up to 3.7 miles (6 km), staying underwater for months at a time, mapping the sea bed. Released from ships, the NOC robots report their findings via a radio link to base on land or water.

ROBO-REPORT
Model: Centauro
Built by: IIT, Italy
Year: 2018
Role: Disaster response
Height: 4.9 feet (1.5 m)
Weight: 205 pounds (93 kg)
Sensors: Cameras, LiDAR, depth, thermal state
Tools: Gripping hands can use human tools

HORSE POWER

Centauro is a lightweight, horse-like robot on four wheels, developed for disaster response. After an earthquake, Centauro can cross piles of rubble, crouch, bend, swivel, and lift obstacles, to reach injured people inside ruined buildings and even smash through doors to reach them. The robot is controlled by a human operator wearing a special full-body **telepresence suit** that allows the operator to see, hear, and "touch" what the robot does as if in an **augmented-reality (AR)** environment.

MOBILE MACHINES

Legs, wheels, wings, and fins – robots are on the move and can even help people get about. Meet the mobile robots and find out how they stop themselves bumping into things.

SUPER SWEEP

Vacuum cleaning can be tiresome, so why not let a robot do it! iRobot's vacuuming **Roomba** navigates its way around furniture and avoids steep drops by using a camera, sensors, and an indoor positioning system. The same sensors can also locate dirt that needs sweeping up. It can remember its path, work out the most efficient route and get back to its recharging station all on its own. The Roomba moves on two side wheels that let it spin around.

ROBO-REPORT
Model: Roomba 966
Built by: iRobot, USA
Year: 2015
Role: Floor sweeper
Weight: 8.8 pounds (4 kg)
Sensors: Touch, infrared, navigation
Tools: Rotating brushes, vacuum suction

SEA SNAKE

For deep-sea inspection duties and repairs, the Norwegian technology group Eelume AS are developing a robot that can work underwater and wriggle into tight spaces like a sea snake. The **Eelume** has a flexible body built of separate units, with sensors and thrusters along its length to safely propel it through the water, plus a light and a gripping tool at the front. It is expected to work down to 1,640 feet (500 m), checking out offshore drilling platforms below the surface.

ROBO-REPORT
Model: SpotMini
Built by: Boston Dynamics, USA
Year: 2019
Role: Various, including construction inspection
Weight: 66 pounds (30 kg) with arm
Height: 2.8 feet (0.84 m)
Tools: Gripping arm

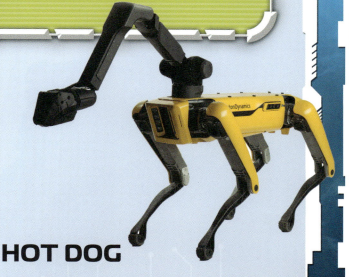

HOT DOG

SpotMini is based on a dog and can walk and run across rough or slippery terrain. SpotMini can carry loads up to 31 pounds (14 kg) and operate for 90 minutes on one battery charge. SpotMini carries front and side cameras plus a "butt cam" and could be used for construction, delivery, or security work.

STEP BY STEP

Robots can also be used to help people move. The **Atlas 2030 exoskeleton** is a wearable robot that has been designed to help children affected by paraplegia, quadraplegia, and spinal problems get about under their own control. If the child has limited movement, the exoskeleton can follow his lead, or it can be controlled with a joystick.

POWER PUP

On a smaller scale, and somewhat cuddlier, Sony's **Aibo** is a robotic pet puppy. The $2,900 toy responds to key words such as sit, play, and shake, and can be trained to play with a ball and be obedient just like a real dog. Aibo has six sensors, a motion detector, a light detector, four microphones, and two cameras that help it remember up to a hundred faces. The pet will learn to find its way around its owner's house and learn new tricks via an app.

BATTLEFIELD BOTS

Could we one day see a war fought solely by machines? Military robots are already in use on the battlefield. While drones are used for surveillance and bomb-delivery, armored patrol robots are guarding borders.

HEAVY DUTY

The **Armored Combat Engineer Robot (ACER)** is a remotely controlled, heavy-duty, bulldozer-sized vehicle. Three different tools can be attached to the front: a mechanical arm for removing explosive devices, a cutter for grabbing or chopping away obstacles, and a plow for clearing a path. This military vehicle is also used to help fight fires.

SUIT UP

The XOS-2 exoskeleton uses high-pressure hydraulics to amplify the wearer's strength allowing him to smash through barriers and lift weights up to 198 pounds (90 kg) with ease.

ROBO-REPORT
Model: Armored Combat Engineer Robot (ACER)
Built by: Mesa Robotics, USA
Year: 2006
Role: Clearing paths and explosives
Weight: 4,497 pounds (2,040 kg)
Speed: 6.2 mp (10 kph)
Tools: Manipulator arm, cutter, plow

ROBO-REPORT
Model: XOS-2 exoskeleton
Built by: Raytheon, USA
Year: 2010
Role: Increasing soldiers' strength
Weight: 198 pounds (90 kg)
Sensors: Motion sensors in joints
Tools: Mechanical pincers

BATTLEFIELD BEAR

The **Battlefield Extraction-Assist Robot (BEAR)** is a military robot, developed by the American company Vecna Technologies in 2005, to help rescue wounded soldiers from the battlefield. The robot has a camera and microphone, allowing an operator to control it remotely with spoken commands or a motion-capture device called an **iGlove**. When BEAR reaches a wounded soldier, the robot uses hydraulics to scoop them up and move them to a safe place.

ROUGH STUFF

The **Dragon Runner** wheeled combat robot is built to survive the toughest duties in urban combat. Just 20 pounds (9 kg) in weight, the Dragon Runner can be carried and even thrown from a moving vehicle or third floor window. The robot is remotely controlled via **WiFi** and video camera to check out hostile territory. Its on-board sensors can also detect movement up to 30 feet (9 m) away, while its extending arm can help defuse roadside explosives.

TECH TANK

The **Modular Advanced Armed Robotic System (MAARS)** is a miniature robot tank in development for the US military for reconnaissance, surveillance, and scouting targets. The robot is built to support patrols and comes with a loudspeaker for issuing commands. It can be armed with a machine gun and four grenade launchers, which can only be fired by its human controllers.

ROBO-REPORT
Model: Modular Advanced Armed Robotic System (MAARS)
Built by: QinetQ, USA
Year: 2008
Role: Reconnaissance, surveillance, and target acquisition
Weight: 350 pounds (159 kg)
Speed: 6.8 mph (11 kph)
Sensors: Day and night cameras, motion and hostile-fire detectors
Tools: Manipulator arm, loudspeaker, machine gun, four grenade launchers

MOTOR INDUSTRY

Ever since Unimate joined the assembly line in 1954, factories have been looking at ways to make production safer, quicker, and cheaper with robotic workers. There are over one-and-a-half million industrial robots working in factories today.

ARMY OF ARMS

Most industrial robots are robotic arms that follow repeated programs, picking up and placing objects, welding, spray-painting, and testing products. They can repeat the same task accurately, without tiring or needing rest. The motor industry is the largest user of robotic technology.

ROBO-REPORT
Model: YuMi
Built by: ABB Robotics, Switzerland
Year: 2015
Role: Small-parts assembly
Height: 22 inches (56 cm)
Weight: 83.8 pounds (38 kg)
Sensors: Camera
Tools: Two arms, replaceable grippers

FACE FRONT

Sometimes it's good to see the face of your co-worker. **Sawyer** is a compact, one-armed robot with a screen that displays a mood. Sawyer's multi-jointed, twisting arm can reach 4.1 feet (1.26 m) and repeat tasks, such as metal stamping, packing, and quality control, with utmost precision. But if it does make a rare mistake, Sawyer will display a sad face.

TAKING ORDERS

Online retailer Amazon uses **Kiva** robots in its mammoth fulfilment centers to find orders and prepare them for packing and delivery. They are helped by one of the world's largest robot arms, the **robo-stow**. Amazon has more than 45,000 kivas, working day and night, moving shelves of goods four times their weight around warehouses.

ROBO-REPORT
Model: Kiva
Built by: Amazon Robotics, USA
Year: 2005
Role: Delivery
Weight: 243 pounds (110 kg)
Speed: 2.98 mph (4.8 kph)
Sensors: Navigation
Tools: Barcode scanner, lifting mechanism

SIDE BY SIDE

Cobots are collaborative robots that work alongside humans. **YuMi** – which stands for You and Me – is one example. Its two arms can perform highly accurate and delicate tasks, even folding paper planes thousands of times without a mistake. With a padded body and quick-reaction off switch, this robot can work safely, assembling small parts next to human workers, and can even make cups of coffee!

SHARING THE LOAD

While robots are doing some of the heavy lifting in car factories, humans are managing lighter work with wearable robotic technology. At the German car manufacturer Audi, workers have been testing lightweight **exoskeletons** that help take the load off them during the working day. These wearable robots weigh just 6.6 pounds (3 kg) and fit like clothing, covering the upper body and thighs.

The American car manufacturer General Motors and the American space agency NASA have been working on similar robo-tech to help save workers effort, inventing the **Robo-Glove** to multiply a worker's gripping force, helping them to use tools for long hours with less effort.

ROBOT REPLACEMENTS

Is there a limit to the kind of jobs robots can do? The factory isn't the only place you'll find machines taking over human roles. Here are some very different examples of hard-working robots.

ROBO-REPORT
Model: AnBot
Built by: National Defence University, China
Year: 2016
Role: Security
Weight: 172 pounds (78 kg)
Speed: 11 mph (18 kph)
Sensors: 4 HD cameras, audio recorders, air quality, temperature
Tools: Video screen, taser

MOVING MOUNTAINS

In Australia, huge Caterpillar dump trucks are being used to collect and transport iron ore across the country, but there's no one behind the wheel! These self-driving, 416-ton (377 mt) robot trucks use GPS, radar, and laser sensors to navigate, picking up the ore and taking it to a new site. Their operators are based 746 miles (1,200 km) away, with no need to visit remote mining sites.

COMPUTER COP

The **AnBot** is China's own robot police officer. It patrols an airport in Shenzhen, and while it may look non-threatening, it's programmed for crime-fighting and riot control, can move at 11 mph (18 kph), and is armed with a stun weapon. Anbot's **AI** can also recognize faces and match them with a database of criminals.

SMOOTH OPERATOR

Helping surgeons perform the most delicate operations, the **Da Vinci Surgical System** is a remote-control system that can move surgical instruments to within a fraction of a millimeter, much more accurately than a human could. A surgeon directs the robot using hand and pedal controls, while receiving 3D camera images. The machine has proved itself many times over, with more than 4,000 Da Vinci machines performing more than three million operations since 2000.

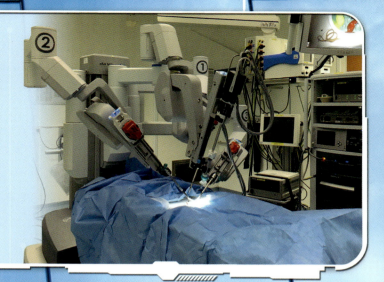

ROBO-REPORT
Model: GEKKO Facade
Built by: Serbot, Switzerland
Year: 2015
Role: Window cleaner
Weight: 154 pounds (70 kg)
Sensors: Navigation
Tools: Suction cups, arms with rotating brushes

CLEAN MACHINE

Cleaning the windows of skyscrapers is not a job for anyone afraid of heights. Thankfully, the **GEKKO Facade** robot window cleaner doesn't even notice the drop from the top floor. This robot cleaning machine slides up buildings on an automated winch and uses rotating brushes to polish glass. It can clean 9,568 square yards (8,000 sq m) of windows every day.

MECHA MENU

Would you trust a robot to rustle up a tasty meal? Though the robot chef doesn't have taste buds, the **Moley Robotic Kitchen** can cook for you by mimicking the moves of a professional chef and using sensors and cameras to deliver a dish from a library of recipes. Ingredients have to be measured and placed in special containers before the robo-chef can start work, though.

AWESOME ANDROIDS

Androids are robots with a human form. While some are built to educate and appeal to children, others are designed to closely resemble people, with synthetic skin, facial expressions, and even a sense of humor.

WALKIE TALKIE

In 1973 Japanese inventor **Ichiro Kato** introduced **WABOT I**, the first human-scale, intelligent, human-shaped robot, or **android**. It could move its own limbs, see its environment, transport objects, and even talk in Japanese. It was thought to have the mental ability of an 18-month-old child.

CHILD'S PLAY

The **iPal** is a robot designed as a playmate and teaching tool for young children. Able to speak, sing, dance, and play games, such as rock/paper/scissors, the iPal has an inbuilt touchscreen loaded with educational games. The robot can help autistic children learn social skills, and act as a nanny too; its eye cameras can share video with parents.

ROBO-REPORT
Model: iPal
Built by: AvatarMind, China
Year: 2016
Role: Education
Height: 3.3 feet (1 meter)
Weight: 29 pounds (13 kg)
Sensors: Cameras, collision avoidance
Tools: Touchscreen, moving arms

GOAL SCORER

It shoots! It scores! **Nao** are android robots that can play soccer, dance, and get up if they fall over. Nao robots have more than fifty sensors to help them find their way around a room. They have been used for teaching and providing customer service.

ROBO-REPORT
Model: Nao
Built by: Aldebaran Robotics, France
Year: 2006
Role: Education
Height: 23 inches (58 cm)
Weight: 12.1 pounds (5.5 kg)
Sensors: 2 HD cameras, microphones, infrared and sonar rangefinders, tactile and pressure
Tools: Moving arms and legs

CHAT-SHOW QUEEN

Sophia is a realistic female humanoid that can produce human-like responses and fifty facial expressions. She even has a sense of humor. Created by Hong Kong-based Hanson Robotics, Sophia is controlled by **artificial intelligence (AI)** with voice-recognition software to respond to questions and continue conversations. Activated in 2016, Sophia is already a media star, having appeared on many science and chat shows around the world. She's even been the cover star of Brazil's *Elle* magazine.

OFF AND RUNNING

Atlas is a super-agile android robot. With 28 hydraulically driven joints, it can walk upright on two legs. Just like a human, it can balance itself as it leans forward to walk and can even get up on its own if it falls over. The designers are working on an upgrade that can jog, leap, and even do backflips!

ROBO-REPORT
Model: Atlas
Built by: Boston Dynamics, USA
Year: 2013
Role: Rescue
Weight: 165 pounds (75 kg)
Height: 4.9 feet (1.5 m)
Sensors: LiDAR and stereo vision
Tools: Lifting arms

23

MECHANICAL MEGASTARS

Racing on the track, shooting flames, and traveling into the deep cosmos, robots are achieving great things.

ROBOT RACER

One of the fastest robots on four legs is the aptly named **Cheetah**. Cheetah has a top speed of 28 mph (45.5 kph) and can even jump over hurdles. While this is close to the speed of a record-breaking human sprinter, it's way behind a living cheetah, which run between 62 and 75 mph (100 to 120 kph).

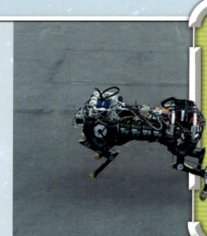

ROBO-REPORT
Model: Cheetah
Built by: MIT, USA
Year: 2012
Role: Inspection and Rescue Robot
Weight: 70.5 pounds (32 kg)
Speed: 28 mph (45.5 kph)
Sensors: Touch

SCIENCE FANTASY

The world's largest walking robot looks like something from a fantasy film. It is 49 feet (15 m) long, 11 ton (10 mt) fire-breathing dragon! The radio-controlled monster machine, named **Tradinno**, was built for the theater and can flap its wings and breathe fire from its mouth and nostrils.

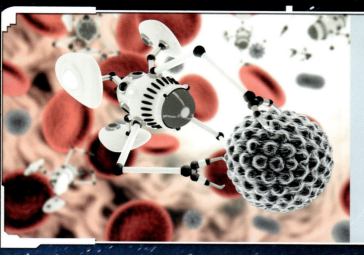

MICRO MEDICS

Impossible to see with the naked eye, tiny **nanobots** could provide a breakthrough in healthcare. At only 120 nanometres across (one nanometre is a millionth of a millimetre) the tiny machines – nanocomposite particles – are controlled by an electromagnetic field to interact with a body's cells. They could deliver medication to cancerous cells and even move them to different locations.

FINAL FRONTIER

Launched in 1977, **Voyager 1** is a robot spacecraft designed to explore Jupiter and Saturn. Currently traveling in interstellar space, it is the human-made object furthest from Earth. Aboard the nuclear-powered Voyager 1 are two gold discs carrying sounds and images from Earth should it ever encounter extraterrestrials.

VIRTUAL VIRTUOSO

The car manufacturer Toyota is developing human-assisting robots for domestic duties and nursing care. To show off the dexterity of their designs, in 2007 they built a robot that could play the violin. With seventeen joints in its hands and arms, the robot could even produce a wavering vibrato sound on the instrument.

ROBO-REPORT
Model: Tradinno
Built by: Zoliner Elektronik AG, Germany
Year: 2010
Role: Theatre
Height: 40.4 feet (12.3 m)
Weight: 12.1 tons (11 mt)
Speed: 1.1 mph (1.8 kph)
Sensors: 238 motion sensors
Tools: Animated legs, tail, wings

ELECTRIC DREAMS

Robots, for good or evil, have played a major part in science fiction, which has shaped the way we think of them. The author Isaac Asimov even came up with a series of rules for robot behavior.

SILVER SIREN

Fritz Lang's 1927 ground-breaking silent film **Metropolis** showed a future where workers were almost robotic. In the tale, a scientist creates a female robot, which he names **Maria**, to control the labor force.

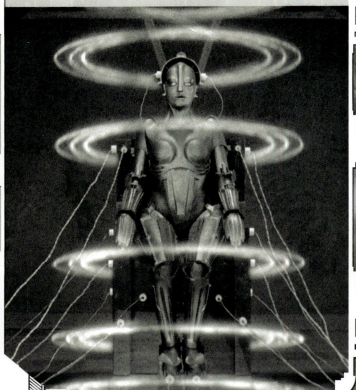

DROID DOUBLE ACT

1977's **Star Wars** droids **C-3PO** and **R2-D2** were the comedy act in the science-fantasy film, often getting into trouble. The droids were given human personalities, with C-3PO the boastful worrier and R2-D2 his stubborn partner. Later Star Wars films introduced viewers to a new, spirited droid named **BB-8**.

THREE LAWS

In his short story "Runaround" (1942) the US author **Isaac Asimov** wrote his **Three Laws of Robotics** – all very sensible ideas for programming automatons. They were:

1. A robot may not injure a human being or, through inaction, allow a human being to come to harm.
2. A robot must obey the orders given it by human beings except where such orders would conflict with the First Law.
3. A robot must protect its own existence as long as such protection does not conflict with the First or Second Laws.

Asimov's stories inspired the 2004 film **I, Robot**, where a robot is deliberately freed from the laws to commit murder.

WALL-E

WALL-E is the computer-animated star of a 2008 Pixar film. Set in the 29th century, Earth has become a garbage-strewn, polluted wasteland. Humanity is nowhere to be found, having had to evacuate to go and live on giant spaceships seven centuries earlier. The only thing still working on Earth is a robot trash-compactor, named WALL-E, left behind to clean up.

THE NEXT UPGRADE

What will robots be like in the future? Will they take away the most boring jobs or could they take over and use humans as slaves? Will robots be our new best friends or our rulers? Here are some possible outcomes.

ROBOT ASTRONAUTS

NASA's **R5 Valkyrie**, developed in 2013, is the astronaut of the future. This two-legged robot could be sent to Mars ahead of a human-led flight, to set up a base and life-support systems. With no need for food, water, or air, the battery-powered robot can do many tasks a human can, including driving, climbing a ladder, and operating tools.

ROBO-REPORT
Model: R5 Valkyrie
Year: 2013
Role: Robot astronaut
Weight: 300 pounds (136 kg)
Computer: 2x Intel Core i7
Sensors: MultiSense SL head camera with laser, 3D stereo and video
Tools: Each three-fingered hand has 38 sensors

CLOUD CONTROL

uture robots may no longer just rely on their own experiences to learn, but those of other robots, and humans too, by connecting online. **Cloud-based** software will allow robots to upgrade and find the answer to new questions without the need for a human to provide updates. A new **RoboNet** could be created with robots sharing information online.

TECH TAKEOVER

Another possible future has robots advancing faster than we can keep up and seeing humans as a problem that needs to be fixed. The military are using lethal robots but they are controlled by humans. What would happen if robots made that choice? Would they turn on us?

FUTURE FRIENDS

As robots gain better communication and social skills, they could even become our friends. Robots are already working as educational playmates for children and as care-givers for elderly patients. Advances in **artificial Intelligence** could lead to robots with consciousness and their own rights to be protected.

CYBORG RACE

Could replacing our body parts with robotic ones help us live longer? People with missing limbs are already benefiting from bionic limb replacements, while retinal implants are restoring vision to people with sight deficiencies. **Cyborgs** are beings with both organic and mechanical parts. Will half-human/half-machine people be a common sight in coming years? Could you turn into a robot?

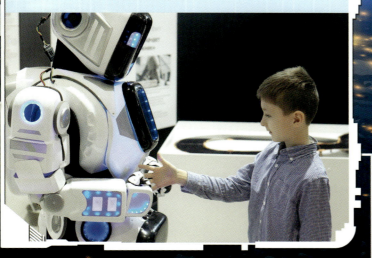

GLOSSARY

Actuator machine component that controls movement

Android robot with human appearance

Artificial intelligence (AI) intelligence demonstrated by machines

Augmented reality (AR) experience of computer-generated environment

Automaton mechanical imitation of a human being

Autonomous able to perform tasks by itself

Bionic having a mechanical body part

Central Processing Unit (CPU) microprocessor, part of computer that controls operations

Cloud-based internet-based

Cybernetics the science of human and machine communication

Cyborg human being with mechanical parts built into the body

Exoskeleton external skeleton, organic or mechanical

Global Positioning System (GPS) a system that can show the exact position of a person or thing by using signals from satellites

Humanoid a machine or creature with the appearance and qualities of a human

Hydraulics the use of liquids to produce power and movement

Light detection and ranging (LiDAR) detection system that reflects lasers to sense what is ahead

Nanobot microscopic robot

Ore rock or soil from which metal can be obtained

Reconnaissance military observation of an area

RoboNet internet used for robot communication

Robot moving machine programmed for specific tasks

Sensor device that receives information about its environment

Simultaneous Localization and Mapping (SLAM) program for mapping unknown area while marking position

Sonar a detection system that measures the echo of sound pulses

Stream to listen to or watch sound or video on a computer directly from the internet rather than downloading it and saving it first

Submersible a type of ship that can travel underwater, especially one that operates without people being in it

Swarm large group

Telepresence technology that allows users to feel like they are present in a remote location

WiFi wire-free technology which uses radio waves to allow devices to link to the internet

Winch a machine that lifts heavy objects by turning a chain or rope around a tube-shaped device

FOR MORE INFORMATION

WEBSITES

Guide to World of Robotics
Robotics news from the Institute of Electrical and Electronics Engineers (IEEE): robots.ieee.org

LEGO Mindstorms
Build a robot site: lego.com/mindstorms/build-a-robot

Popular Mechanics
Articles on robots from a long-running science magazine: popularmechanics.com/technology/robots/

Robots.nu
Information about robots in our lives: www.robots.nu

TED Recommends
Talks about robots: www.ted.com/topics/robots

Science Kids: Robots
Check out the exciting world of robots through fun games, interesting facts, awesome projects, cool quizzes, amazing videos and more: http://www.sciencekids.co.nz/robots.html

BOOKS

A Robot World, Clive Gifford (Franklin Watts, 2017)

DKfindout! Robots, (DK Children, 2018)

Adventures in STEAM: Robots, Izzi Howell (Wayland, 2017)

Kid Engineer: Working with Computers and Robotics, Sonya Newland (Wayland, 2020)

INDEX

A
Aibo 8, 15
AnBot 20
android
    Atlas 9, 23
    iPal 22
    Nao 9, 23
    R5 Valkyrie 9, 28
    WABOT I 8, 22
Archytas 6
Armored Combat Engineer Robot (ACER) 16
arms, robotic 4, 11, 18–19
    Da Vinci Surgical System 9, 11, 21
    iCub 11
    Sawyer 18
    Unimate 8–9, 18
    YuMi 18–19
Asimov, Isaac 26–27
    Three Laws of Robotics 27
automatons 6–7

B
Battlefield Extraction-Assist Robot (BEAR) 17

C
Capek, Karel 4
Centauro 13
Cheetah 24
cobots 19
cyborgs 29

D
Devol, George 9
Dragon Runner 17
drones, military robot 5, 16

E
Eelume 14

exoskeletons, robot
    Atlas 2030 exoskeleton 15
    Robo-Gloves 19
    XOS-2 exoskeleton 16

F
films 26–27

G
GEKKO Facade 21

H
humanoids
    Sophia 23

J
Jaquet-Droz, Pierre 7

K
karakuri 7
Kato, Ichiro 22
Kiva (Amazon) 9, 19

L
Luigi 13

M
MAARS (Modular Advanced Armed Robotic System) 17
microbots 5
Moley Robotic Kitchen 21

N
nanobots 5, 25
NASA rovers
    Curiosity 5, 9
    Mars 2020 9
    Opportunity 9
    Pathfinder 8–9
    Sojourner 8–9

P
PackBots 9, 12

R
robots
    brief history of 4–5
    cleaning robots 4, 9, 14, 21
    disaster-response robots 12–13, 16–17, 24
    human-assisting 25, 29
    human-like 4, 8–9, 11
    medical robots 5, 9, 11, 21, 25, 29
    military robots 5, 12–13, 16–17, 29
    parts of a robot 10–11
    providing security 4, 20
    submarines 13
    toys 4, 8, 15, 22–23
    trucks 20
    used in space 4–5, 8–9, 25, 28
Roomba 9, 14

S
Shakey 8–9
SpotMini 15
Su Song 6

T
Tradinno 24

V
Vaucanson, Jacques de 7
Vinci, Leonardo da 7

W
Walter, William Grey 8